D0772633

ARCTIC FOXES

by Vicky Franchino

Children's Press®

An Imprint of Scholastic Inc.
New York Toronto London Auckland Sydney
Mexico City New Delhi Hong Kong
Danbury, Connecticut

Content Consultant
Dr. Stephen S. Ditchkoff
Professor of Wildlife Sciences
Auburn University
Auburn, Alabama

Photographs © 2014: age fotostock/Arndt Sven-Erik/Arterra Picture
Library: 39; Alamy Images: 35 (Adam Jones/Danita Delimont), 19
(Arctos Images), 27 (Arndt Sven-Erik/Arterra Picture Library), 7, 11 (James
Urbach/SuperStock); Bob Italiano: 44 foreground, 45 foreground;
Dreamstime: 32 (Eric Gevaert), 2 background, 3 background, 44
background, 45 background (John Siebert), 2 foreground, 46 (Mirceax),
36 (Tzooka); Getty Images: 5 top, 15 (Enrique Aguirre), 24 (Konrad
Wothe/Minden Pictures), 20 (Norbert Rosing/National Geographic),
12 (Steven Kazlowski), cover (Wayne Lynch/All Canada Photos);
Media Bakery: 1, 8 (Sohns), 23 (Steven Kazlowski); Photo Researchers/
Jeffrey Lepore: 4, 5 background, 16; Shutterstock, Inc./basel101658: 9;
Superstock, Inc./Minden Pictures: 5 bottom, 28, 31, 40.

Library of Congress Cataloging-in-Publication Data
Franchino, Vicky.
 Arctic foxes / by Vicky Franchino.
 p. cm.–(Nature's children)
 Summary: "This book details the life and habits of Arctic foxes." –
Provided by publisher.
 Audience: 9–12.
 Audience: Grades 4 to 6.
 Includes bibliographical references and index.
 ISBN 978-0-531-23354-2 (lib. bdg.) – ISBN 978-0-531-25152-2
(pbk.)
 1. Arctic fox–Juvenile literature. 2. Arctic fox–Conservation–Juvenile
literature. I. Title. II. Series: Nature's children (New York, N.Y.)
 QL737.C22F7 2013
 599.776'4–dc23   2013000085

No part of this publication may be reproduced in whole or in part,
or stored in a retrieval system, or transmitted in any form or by any
means, electronic, mechanical, photocopying, recording, or otherwise,
without written permission of the publisher. For information regarding
permission, write to Scholastic Inc., Attention: Permissions Department,
557 Broadway, New York, NY 10012.
© 2014 Scholastic Inc.

All rights reserved. Published in 2014 by Children's Press, an imprint
of Scholastic Inc.

Printed in China 62
SCHOLASTIC, CHILDREN'S PRESS, and associated logos are
trademarks and/or registered trademarks of Scholastic Inc.

1 2 3 4 5 6 7 8 9 10 R 23 22 21 20 19 18 17 16 15 14

Arctic Foxes

Class	Mammalia
Order	Carnivora
Family	Canidae
Genus	*Vulpes*
Species	*Vulpes lagopus*
World distribution	North America, Iceland, Greenland, Siberia, Scandinavian countries
Habitat	Arctic and alpine tundra
Distinctive physical characteristics	Two types of fur: a thick, white or bluish coat in winter and a lighter gray or brown coat in summer; average body length 27 inches (69 centimeters), not including tail; long tail used for warmth and balance; short legs, nose, and ears help conserve body heat; feet are covered in fur
Habits	Male and female sometimes mate for life; both parents care for young; live in underground burrows; bury food supplies to survive in colder temperatures; will sometimes scavenge for food
Diet	Omnivorous; prefer lemmings, voles, birds, eggs, hares, fish, and carrion; will also eat berries, insects, and seaweed

Contents

CHAPTER 1

Life in a Cold, Cold Place

A biting wind sweeps the dark and empty land. There are no trees to block the ferocious gusts and no sun to lend the slightest bit of warmth. Moonlight reflects off the bright white snow that blankets the ground. It might seem as if no creature could survive in this vast tundra. But if you look closely, you might spot the outline of a furry white shape against the snow. It is an Arctic fox, sitting quietly and calmly. The icy expanse looks unwelcoming, but the hardy Arctic fox is right at home.

Most animals could not survive in this harsh and empty environment. But the Arctic fox is built to survive the long winters and short summers of the tundra. It is one of the only mammals found in its habitat.

Arctic foxes seem to disappear completely as they travel through the deep, white snow of their frozen habitat.

All About the Arctic Fox

The Arctic fox is about the size of a large house cat. It is usually around 12 inches (30 centimeters) tall and 27 inches (69 cm) long. This does not include the fox's tail, which can add another 14 inches (36 cm) to its length. The Arctic fox typically weighs between 7 and 21 pounds (3 and 9.5 kilograms). Males are bigger than females.

Like all foxes, the Arctic fox belongs to the canine family. Other animals in this family include wolves, jackals, coyotes, and **domestic dogs**. While other foxes tend to have long legs, ears, and **muzzles**, everything about the Arctic fox is short and squat. Having less surface area makes it easier for the Arctic fox to survive the extreme cold of its habitat. This is because there is less body surface that can be exposed to the cold.

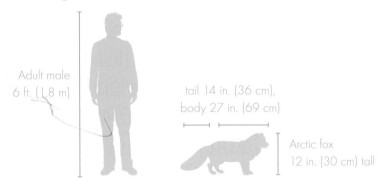

Adult male
6 ft. (1.8 m)

tail 14 in. (36 cm),
body 27 in. (69 cm)

Arctic fox
12 in. (30 cm) tall

An Arctic fox is stockier than other foxes because of its extra-thick layer of fat for warmth.

A Resourceful Creature

Much of the Arctic fox's life is spent searching for food. It eats almost anything it can find. Its diet often includes small rodents such as lemmings and voles, birds, bird eggs, hares, and fish. The Arctic fox sometimes eats berries, insects, and seaweed, too. In the spring, it likes to eat newborn ringed seal pups.

The Arctic fox's favorite food is the lemming. The lemming is so important to the Arctic fox's diet that the species' population usually goes up or down depending on how many lemmings there are.

When the Arctic fox has more food than it needs, it creates food caches for later. The fox digs a natural freezer in the top layer of the frozen soil and stores food inside.

FUN FACT! Some Arctic foxes move food from cache to cache to help them remember where their different hiding spots are located.

An Arctic fox can use its paws and mouth to dig through the snow in search of a tasty meal.

Hunter and Scavenger

During long, cold winters of the Arctic, the sun does not rise for months at a time. The Arctic fox must survive temperatures that can drop to –60 degrees Fahrenheit (–51 degrees Celsius). The Arctic fox doesn't **hibernate**, and it can be hard for the fox to find enough food. Arctic foxes live in territories that cover between 2,100 and 15,000 acres (850 and 6,070 hectares), with most living in territories at the smaller end of that range.

If an Arctic fox can't find enough food in its home **territory**, it might travel hundreds of miles in search of something to eat.

When food is in short supply, the Arctic fox might be forced to **scavenge**. Leftovers from the hunt of a polar bear or wolf are a delicious treat for a hungry Arctic fox. Getting near these meals can be dangerous, though. Polar bears and wolves are the Arctic fox's natural **predators**!

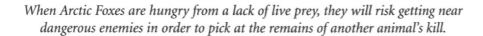

When Arctic Foxes are hungry from a lack of live prey, they will risk getting near dangerous enemies in order to pick at the remains of another animal's kill.

CHAPTER 2

Staying Alive

Like all mammals, the Arctic fox is endothermic. This means it keeps its body temperature roughly the same no matter how cold or warm the outside air is.

The Arctic fox has some special features to help keep it from getting too warm or too cold. One is its fur coat. Before the long, frigid winter arrives, Arctic foxes grow thick, warm fur. Most have a winter coat that is cream colored or white. This is a perfect **camouflage** in the snow. Arctic foxes that live closer to water may have a winter coat that is bluish gray, which blends in with the rocky coastline.

In the summer, the Arctic fox sheds its heavy fur and grows a lightweight coat that is gray or brown. The darker coloring helps the fox blend in with its surroundings. This makes it easier for the Arctic fox to sneak up on its **prey** and helps it hide from predators.

An Arctic fox can look like it has become a completely different animal when its fur changes color for the season.

Feet, Fat, and Food

An Arctic fox's fur completely covers its body. The Arctic fox even has fur on the bottom of its feet! In fact, the scientific name for the Arctic fox is *lagopus*, meaning "hare footed," because hares also have fur on their foot pads. These fuzzy foot pads keep the Arctic fox warm and prevent it from slipping on the ice. A long fluffy tail helps the fox balance and also protects it against the cold.

Not everything that keeps the Arctic fox warm is visible on the outside. One important hidden feature is a layer of body fat. The Arctic fox eats extra food during the summer months to create this protective **insulation**.

The Arctic fox's rate of **metabolism** helps the animal survive in the cold as well. When food is in short supply during the winter months, the Arctic fox moves less, so its body does not need as much energy.

FUN FACT! An Arctic fox's fur is better at keeping heat in and cold out than any other species found in the Arctic.

Furry foot pads help Arctic foxes get a grip as they hop across icy surfaces.

A Unique Way to Keep Warm

A special circulatory system helps the Arctic fox live comfortably on the frozen tundra. The human body is designed to keep the central part of the body warm. If a person is outside for a long time, less blood will flow away from the heart and internal organs. This is why hands and feet get very cold when a person is outside in cold weather. The Arctic fox can't go inside to warm up, so it uses something called countercurrent blood circulation.

In this system, the arteries—which carry warm blood from the heart—flow right next to the veins. Veins carry cooler blood back to the heart. Having the veins and arteries close to each other lets them share their heat and helps keep the whole body warm. Scientists have found that animals such as penguins, dolphins, reindeer, and dogs share this feature.

Arctic foxes often curl up into a ball to help stay warm while they rest.

An Ear to the Ground

The Arctic fox relies on its keen senses to help it survive. For example, it uses its hearing to find food. When a fox is hunting, it stands still and quiet as it listens for approaching prey. When the prey is close, the Arctic fox leaps through the air and pounces on its dinner.

The Arctic fox's hearing is so good that it can even hear animals that are hidden in the snow! During the long winter months, lemmings and voles dig networks of tunnels deep in the snow. The Arctic fox listens carefully to hear the animals burrowing beneath it. This lets the fox know just where to dig to find its next meal!

FUN FACT! A single Arctic fox can eat more than 1,000 bird eggs per year.

As an Arctic fox hops into the air, it tilts its body forward to land front feet first on its prey.

Sharp Senses

Being able to see well both in the dark and in bright light is especially important to the Arctic fox. During the Arctic winter, the sun does not rise for several months. The Arctic fox has excellent night vision, which allows it to find food and avoid danger during this time. The sun shines for most of the day in the summer. In the bright glare of snow and ice, dark **pigment** shades the fox's eyes. This shading acts like a pair of sunglasses. It enables the fox to keep a lookout on even the brightest days.

A strong sense of smell tells the Arctic fox when prey is near. It also helps the fox find its hidden food caches. The Arctic fox counts on the fact that other foxes also have a strong sense of smell. It uses its urine and droppings to mark its territory and tell other foxes to "stay away."

Arctic foxes often sniff along the ground to catch the scent of prey as they search for food.

Call of the Wild

The Arctic fox is not a very vocal animal, but it sometimes uses its voice during courtship or to communicate with its offspring or with foxes outside its family. The tone of an Arctic fox's call is important. A parent might make a yelping sound when its kits are in danger or a chittering sound when it is returning to its young in the den. If an Arctic fox wants to warn another fox to stay out of its territory, it often uses a high-pitched whine. Sometimes it makes a noise that sounds more like a scream or a hiss.

The Arctic fox communicates in other ways, too. During courtship, it might move its tail or ears in a certain way. The male and female might also chase or fight with each other to show they are interested in mating.

FUN FACT! In Alaska, around 4,000 Arctic foxes are killed for their fur each year.

Sounds are one of the many ways that Arctic foxes communicate with one another.

CHAPTER 3

All in the Family

During spring and summer, Arctic fox families live together in underground dens. These dens are often built in hillsides. The foxes find areas of sandy soil where it is easier to dig through the frozen ground. Most Arctic fox families use the same den year after year.

Some dens have many different rooms with tunnels between them. The Arctic fox is always careful to build more than one way out of the den. If there is a sign of danger in one area, the Arctic fox can escape another way. Some dens have as many as 100 exits!

As the weather begins to cool down in fall, the fox family members leave the den to spend winters hunting alone. In winter, the Arctic fox sometimes finds itself far from home as it searches for food. Then it might dig into the snow to make a shelter. This might not seem very comfortable, but it is warmer than being in the open air.

An Arctic fox family's summer is filled with the bustling activity of young foxes at play.

Together Through Life

A typical Arctic fox family includes one male (called a reynard), a female (vixen), and their babies (kits). Sometimes the family might include a second vixen. One of the vixens will **breed**, and the other one will help care for the babies.

Arctic foxes are usually **monogamous** and sometimes **mate** for life. Mating usually happens in the spring, and the kits are born around 52 days later. Most **litters** have between 5 and 8 kits, though there have been Arctic fox litters with more than 20 babies. Usually more kits are born in years when there is plenty of food. Most of the kits will not survive their first year. Sometimes there just isn't enough food for all the kits, and Arctic fox pups are a favorite meal of eagles and wolves.

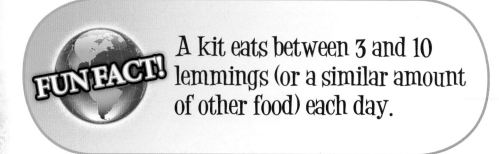

FUN FACT! A kit eats between 3 and 10 lemmings (or a similar amount of other food) each day.

Kits learn valuable hunting skills by wrestling and playing with each other.

Caring for Kits

Kits are completely helpless when they are born. They are blind and deaf, they don't have any teeth, and they only weigh around 2 ounces (57 grams). That is about as much as a candy bar weighs!

During their early days, kits stay in the den and drink milk from their mother. They start to eat meat when they are about a month old.

When the kits are about three months old, they will begin to hunt for themselves. They learn how to hunt by wrestling with their siblings and watching their parents. By the first winter, it is time for the kits to live on their own.

An Arctic fox can start its own family when it is about 10 months old. When spring comes again, the previous year's kits are ready to be the current year's mothers and fathers. In the wild, an Arctic fox's average life expectancy is only about 3 years. In captivity, it might be 10 years or longer.

An Arctic fox mother's milk provides all the nutrition young foxes need during the first few weeks of their lives.

CHAPTER 4

Foxes Around the World

Although the Arctic fox is found only in the far north today, scientists believe it might have lived farther south in the past. Scientists study fossil remains to learn more about an animal's ancestors and where they lived.

Scientists believe that the first ancestors of the modern fox appeared about 55 million years ago, after the dinosaurs disappeared. This animal group is called Carnivora. Nearly 300 current animal species share this ancestor.

Today, foxes are found in every part of the world except Antarctica. Some live near cities, while others live in the wild. Some live in dry deserts, and others are found in cool, wet places.

All foxes have some things in common, such as long bushy tails and claws that can be pulled partway into the toe. They all have excellent hearing and vision as well.

Like Arctic foxes, corsac foxes have fur that is white or gray in the winter and darker during the summer.

American Foxes

Red foxes are found on every continent except Antarctica and South America. Although they are called "red," their fur can actually be a variety of colors. As wild areas disappear, red foxes often end up living near people. They are very good at **adapting** to new environments. When they live near humans, they often rely on garbage for their meals and abandoned buildings for shelter.

Gray foxes live everywhere from southern Canada to South America. They usually live in forests and are the only foxes that can climb trees.

The swift fox certainly lives up to its name. It can run at speeds close to 40 miles (64 kilometers) per hour. This fox is found on the Great Plains of the United States and in Canada. The species was once in danger of disappearing from some areas, but **conservationists** have worked to increase its population.

After climbing high into the treetops, gray foxes travel by hopping from branch to branch.

Big Ears, Small Bodies

The fennec fox is one of the most unusual looking foxes in the world. It is the smallest type of fox, but it has enormous ears. These ears help the fennec fox survive the brutal temperatures of the Sahara Desert by releasing heat from its body. Like the Arctic fox, the fennec has fur-covered foot pads. But this fur protects the fox's paws from the sand's scorching heat instead of the cold of ice and snow. It also helps the fennec fox to walk on top of the desert sand instead of sinking into it.

The bat-eared fox is another desert dweller with oversized ears. In addition to helping this fox keep cool, these extra-large ears also give it an excellent sense of hearing. This helps the fox to find one of its favorite foods—termites. The bat-eared fox likes to live near larger animals like buffalo and wildebeests because they kick up bugs when they move around.

Each of a fennec fox's ears is around 6 inches (15 centimeters) long.

CHAPTER 5

Protecting the Arctic Fox

Throughout history, hunting has been the biggest threat to the Arctic fox. Its warm fur has been highly valued for clothing. In some Scandinavian countries, it was hunted almost to extinction. Over the years, it has become less popular to use fur for clothing. As a result, hunting has become less of a concern.

Unfortunately, Arctic foxes face a new menace: climate change. The earth has been slowly warming over time. In recent decades, the rate of warming has increased rapidly. As the planet grows warmer, the Arctic fox will face a number of threats.

One is that its food supply might disappear. The Arctic fox's main food source is lemmings. During the winter, lemmings rely on snowbanks for warmth and to protect the plants they feed on. If the weather is too warm to support this protective snow covering, the lemmings may not survive.

Arctic foxes need a healthy population of lemmings,
like the one in this fox's mouth, to survive.

The Dangers of Climate Change

Climate change could also result in fewer places where polar bears and ringed seals can live. The Arctic fox often relies on the polar bear's leftovers in the winter, and the ringed seal is a common food source in late spring. Without these animals, the Arctic fox could starve.

Another threat is a change in habitat. As the land grows warmer, the tundra may turn into a forest. The Arctic fox cannot live in this environment. Warmer temperatures are also causing red foxes to move north. The two fox species compete for food and resources. The problem will only grow worse if more red foxes move into Arctic fox habitats.

How can people help the Arctic fox? Countries such as Norway and Sweden have laws in place to prevent hunting. In addition, some organizations have begun captive breeding programs. These programs allow Arctic foxes to mate and produce babies in protected environments. Efforts such as these will help prevent these fantastic foxes from disappearing forever.

Because of climate change, red foxes and Arctic foxes now live and hunt in some of the same areas.

Words to Know

adapting (uh-DAPT-ing) — changing to fit a new setting or set of circumstances

ancestors (AN-ses-turz) — ancient animal species that are related to modern species

breed (BREED) — to mate and give birth to young

caches (CASH-iz) — places for hiding food or supplies

camouflage (KAM-uh-flahzh) — a disguise or a natural coloring that allows animals, people, or objects to hide by making them look like their surroundings

captivity (kap-TIV-i-tee) — the condition of being held or trapped by people

conservationists (kon-sur-VAY-shun-ists) — people who work to protect an environment and the living things in it

courtship (KORT-ship) — the process in which an animal expresses its interest in mating

domestic (duh-MES-tik) — animals that have been tamed; people use them as a source of food or as work animals, or keep them as pets

fossil (FAH-suhl) — a bone, shell, or other trace of an animal or plant from millions of years ago, preserved as rock

habitat (HAB-uh-tat) — the place where an animal or a plant is usually found

hibernate (HYE-bur-nate) — to spend the entire winter sleeping or resting; hibernation helps animals survive when temperatures are cold and food is hard to find

insulation (in-suh-LAY-shun) — something that prevents heat from escaping

litters (LIT-urz) — groups of baby animals that are born at the same time to the same mother

mammals (MAM-uhlz) — warm-blooded animals that have hair or fur and usually give birth to live babies; female mammals produce milk to feed their young

mate (MATE) — to join together to produce babies

metabolism (muh-TAB-uh-liz-uhm) — the rate at which an animal uses energy

monogamous (mah-NAH-guh-mus) — having only one mate

muzzles (MUHZ-uhlz) — animals' noses and mouths

pigment (PIG-muhnt) — a substance that gives color to something

predators (PRED-uh-turz) — animals that live by hunting other animals for food

prey (PRAY) — an animal that's hunted by another animal for food

scavenge (SCAV-uhnj) — to feed on kills left behind by other animals

species (SPEE-sheez) — one of the groups into which animals and plants of the same genus are divided; members of the same species can mate and have offspring

territory (TER-i-tor-ee) — area of land claimed by an animal

tundra (TUHN-druh) — a very cold area of northern Europe, Asia, and Canada where there are no trees and the soil under the surface of the ground is always frozen

Habitat Map

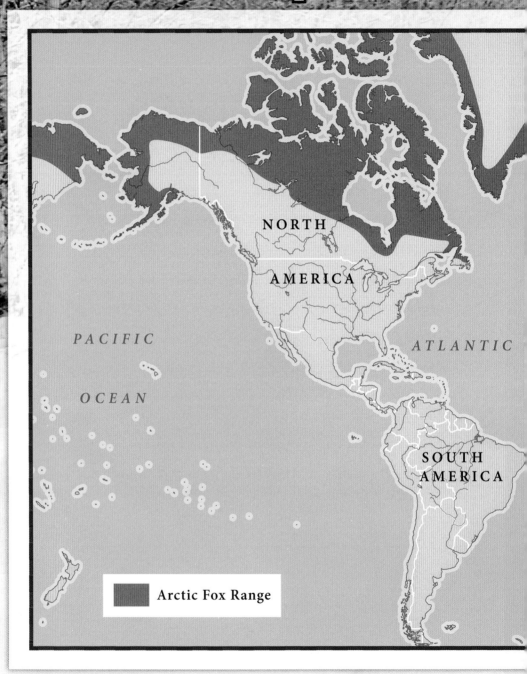

NORTH

AMERICA

PACIFIC

OCEAN

ATLANTIC

SOUTH
AMERICA

Arctic Fox Range

ARCTIC OCEAN

EUROPE

ASIA

AFRICA

PACIFIC OCEAN

INDIAN

OCEAN

CEAN

AUSTRALIA

45

Find Out More

Books

Lynch, Wayne. *Arctic A to Z.* Richmond Hill, ON, CAN: Firefly Books, 2009.

Owen, Ruth. *Arctic Fox Pups.* New York: Bearport Publishing, 2011.

Person, Stephen. *Arctic Fox: Very Cool!* New York: Bearport Publishing, 2009.

Visit this Scholastic Web site for more information on Arctic foxes:
www.factsfornow.scholastic.com
Enter the keywords **Arctic foxes**

Index

About the Author

Vicky Franchino is not a big fan of winter and can't imagine living somewhere as cold as the Arctic! She is glad that Arctic foxes have so many special features to help them survive in the harsh climate of the far, far north. Vicky prefers indoor heating! She has written dozens of books for children and thinks that it's fascinating to learn about different types of animals. She lives in Madison, Wisconsin, with her husband and daughters.
Photo by Kat Franchino

CONTRA COSTA COUNTY LIBRARY
31901055354759